AF228604

CHECKERBOARD BIOGRAPHIES

ARETHA FRANKLIN

JESSICA RUSICK

**Checkerboard
Library**

An Imprint of Abdo Publishing
abdobooks.com

ABDOBOOKS.COM

Published by Abdo Publishing, a division of ABDO, PO Box 398166, Minneapolis, Minnesota 55439.
Copyright © 2022 by Abdo Consulting Group, Inc. International copyrights reserved in all countries.
No part of this book may be reproduced in any form without written permission from the publisher.
Checkerboard Library™ is a trademark and logo of Abdo Publishing.

Printed in the United States of America, North Mankato, Minnesota
052021
092021

Design and Production: Mighty Media, Inc.
Editor: Liz Salzmann
Cover Photograph: Harry Langdon/Getty Images
Interior Photographs: Atlantic Records/Wikimedia Commons, pp. 13, 28 (bottom); Charles Sykes/AP Images, pp. 5, 29 (bottom right); Dave Brinkman (ANEFO)/Wikimedia Commons, p. 9; DP/AP Images, pp. 15, 28 (top right); Library of Congress, p. 19; Mike Albans/AP Images, pp. 23, 29 (top); MSgt Cecilio Ricardo/Wikimedia Commons, pp. 25, 29; RCA Victor Records/Wikimedia Commons, p. 11; Shutterstock Images, pp. 13 (paper clip), 27; The Estate of David Gahr/Getty Images, p. 17; Thomas R Machnitzki/Wikimedia Commons, pp. 7, 28; 3629377Globe Photos/MediaPunch/AP Images, p. 21

Library of Congress Control Number: 2021932873

Publisher's Cataloging-in-Publication Data
Names: Rusick, Jessica, author.
Title: Aretha Franklin / by Jessica Rusick
Description: Minneapolis, Minnesota : Abdo Publishing, 2022 | Series: Checkerboard biographies | Includes online resources and index.
Identifiers: ISBN 9781532195983 (lib. bdg.) | ISBN 9781098216849 (ebook)
Subjects: LCSH: Franklin, Aretha--Juvenile literature. | Women singers--United States--Biography--Juvenile literature. | Soul musicians--United States--Biography--Juvenile literature. | African American women singers--Biography--Juvenile literature. | Actors and actresses--Biography--Juvenile literature. | Civil rights workers--Biography--Juvenile literature.
Classification: DDC 782.421644--dc23

CONTENTS

CHAPTER 1

THE QUEEN OF SOUL

Aretha Franklin was a singer, pianist, and civil rights activist. She was known for her emotional singing. Her talent led many to call her the "Queen of Soul."

Franklin's career lasted 60 years. She released more than 40 albums. She started as a **gospel** singer. But she became famous in the 1960s for **secular** soul music. Many of her hit songs are now considered classics. In later years, she continued to give performances that brought **audiences** to their feet.

Franklin earned many awards and honors over her long career. But Franklin also faced tragedy in her life, including the deaths of relatives. Music kept Franklin going through tough times.

Franklin spent her childhood surrounded by music. Her parents were friends with the greatest singers of their age. Franklin grew up learning from legends. One day, she would become one herself.

Franklin performed and recorded many different styles of music during her career.

A HOUSE FULL OF MUSIC

Aretha Louise Franklin was born in Memphis, Tennessee, on March 25, 1942. She had four **siblings**. Her father, Clarence, or C.L., was a pastor. Her mother, Barbara, was a **gospel** singer and pianist.

When Aretha was four, her family moved to Detroit, Michigan. C.L. had gotten a job preaching at a local church. He was known for his passionate sermons, which often included singing. His church, and Aretha's home, were at the center of a strong African American community.

When Aretha was six, her parents separated. Aretha's mother moved to Buffalo, New York. Aretha and her siblings stayed with their father.

PLAYING BY EAR

When her father hired a piano teacher, Aretha hid so she wouldn't have to take lessons! She preferred to learn by ear. Later in life, she said that playing by ear let her "develop a rather personal and signature style, which I treasure and would not give up for anything or anyone."

Franklin's birthplace in Memphis

C.L.'s house was nearly always filled with music. He was friends with many famous **gospel** singers including Mahalia Jackson and Clara Ward. They were like family to Aretha. When she heard their passionate performances, Aretha knew she wanted to be a singer too.

C.L. encouraged all his children to be musical. But he was especially impressed by young Aretha's talent. When she was nine, her father encouraged her to sing her first **solo** at church. She was nervous, but churchgoers were blown away by her powerful voice. It was clear that Aretha had a gift for singing.

In 1952, Aretha's mother died suddenly from a heart attack. Aretha was stunned by the loss. Even years later, she could not describe the pain she felt when she heard the news. Aretha channeled her pain into her singing.

There was always music in our house. The radio was going in one room, the record player in another, the piano banging away in the living room.

Jackson is considered one of the most important gospel singers of the 1900s. She performed concerts around the world.

CHAPTER 3

ON TOUR

Aretha started performing on the road when she was 12 years old. During summers, she toured the country with her father and many of his **gospel**-singer friends. Aretha played piano and sang gospel songs just as she did at her father's church. For the first time, **audiences** around the country heard the power and range of Aretha's voice.

Traveling could be difficult. Aretha's group played some shows in the South. At the time, the South had **segregation** laws. So, Aretha's group couldn't go to bars and hotels that were for "whites only."

Life on the road was difficult for other reasons. Aretha had two sons, Clarence and Edward. While Aretha was on tour, her children lived with her grandmother. Aretha visited when she could.

While on tour, Aretha met singer Sam Cooke. Like Aretha, Cooke started as a gospel singer. But when he switched to **secular** music, he became more popular. Aretha longed to reach a wider audience too.

Cooke was just 33 years old when he died. Although his career was short, his music was very influential. He is often called the "King of Soul."

CHAPTER 4

STRUGGLES & SUCCESSES

Watching Cooke's rise to fame inspired the next stage of Franklin's career. In 1960, Franklin told her father she wanted to sing **secular** music. Some **gospel** fans thought secular music was **immoral** because it did not have religious themes. But Franklin's father liked all music. He gave Franklin his support.

Franklin moved to New York City. There, she signed a recording contract with Columbia Records. In 1961, Columbia Records released Franklin's first secular album. It was called *Aretha*.

That same year, Franklin married Ted White. He was a Detroit businessman. Not everyone was happy about the marriage. Franklin's father did not trust White. Many considered him to be a controlling person. But Franklin was in love. After the two married, White became Franklin's manager. The couple had a son, Ted Jr., in 1964.

White felt Franklin should switch musical styles from album to album. He thought this would help Franklin

BIO BASICS

NAME: Aretha Louise Franklin

NICKNAMES: Ree; the Queen of Soul

BIRTH: March 25, 1942, Memphis, Tennessee

DEATH: August 16, 2018, Detroit, Michigan

SPOUSES: Ted White (1961-1969); Glynn Turman (1978-1984)

CHILDREN: Clarence, Edward, Ted Jr., Kecalf

FAMOUS FOR: her range and powerful voice; dozens of chart-topping hits and memorable performances

ACHIEVEMENTS: 18 Grammy Awards; first woman inducted into the Rock & Roll Hall of Fame

appeal to a lot of different people. In the following years, Franklin released several more albums with Columbia Records. Franklin sang everything from jazz standards to showtunes.

But instead of attracting listeners, the constant change confused people. Franklin was widely recognized as a talented singer. But she didn't have a musical identity. Franklin later said her albums with Columbia Records were not true to her style.

Soul to me is a feeling, a lot of depth and being able to bring to the surface that which is happening inside, to make the picture clear.

In 1966, Franklin signed with Atlantic Records. Atlantic Records focused on soul music. Soul is raw and emotional, similar to **gospel** music. Franklin felt that soul suited her style.

At Atlantic Records, Franklin had more control over her musical identity. She picked which songs she sang. She also played piano, which she hadn't done since touring with her father years earlier.

Franklin's first album with Atlantic Records came out in 1967. It was called *I Never Loved a Man the Way I Love*

You. The album's title song changed the course of her career. "I Never Loved a Man (The Way I Love You)" became Franklin's first top-ten hit. The song was about a woman's difficult relationship with a man.

Critics and fans admired the way Franklin sang about tough topics. Her voice struck a balance between sorrow and power. The song paved the way for some of Franklin's most famous work.

At Atlantic Records, Franklin worked with producer Jerry Wexler. He is known for being the first to use the term "rhythm & blues" to describe a type of music.

CHAPTER 5

R-E-S-P-E-C-T

The album *I Never Loved a Man the Way I Love You* reached number two on *Billboard*'s top albums chart. It also gave Franklin another hit song, "Respect." The song was originally sung by singer and songwriter Otis Redding. But Franklin made it her own.

This included adding the song's best-known line, "R-E-S-P-E-C-T/Find out what it means to me." Redding's song was about a man begging for respect. Franklin's version was about a woman demanding it.

"Respect" was about two people in a relationship. But Franklin's powerful **vocals** made it about much more. "Respect" soon became an **anthem** for the **civil rights** movement. Since the time of slavery, Black Americans faced **racism** in the United States. Slavery ended in 1865. But **discriminatory** laws existed for many years afterward. Franklin had experienced these unfair laws while touring the South with her father.

> **People want respect— even small children, even babies. As people, we deserve respect from one another.**

Aretha (*left*) and her sister Carolyn working in a studio at Atlantic Records. Carolyn and their sister Erma sang backup vocals on "Respect."

In the 1950s and 60s, Black Americans fought for equal rights. **Activists** such as Dr. Martin Luther King Jr. led marches and protests. They strove to change America's laws.

Franklin's song struck a nerve during this time. Many Black Americans thought "Respect" perfectly represented the respect they demanded. Years later, **civil rights** leader John Lewis spoke of listening to Franklin's music after protests. He said he and other activists would "let the music of Aretha Franklin fill our hearts."

Franklin said she hadn't meant for the song to symbolize a movement. But as a longtime civil rights supporter, she was happy with the association. Franklin continued to support the movement through her music. For years, she performed concerts to raise money for civil rights causes.

Franklin's star rose quickly after "Respect" was released. She became known as the "Queen of Soul." This title would stick for the rest of her career.

King was shot and killed in 1968.
Franklin sang at his memorial service.

CHAPTER 6

RETURN TO GOSPEL

Between 1967 and 1972, Franklin won eight Grammy Awards. Along with her career success, Franklin also experienced changes in her personal life. In 1969, she and White divorced. Soon after, Franklin began dating her tour manager, Ken Cunningham. The two had a son, Kecalf, in 1970.

In 1972, Franklin returned to **gospel** music with the album *Amazing Grace*. The music was recorded live at a church in Los Angeles, California. Franklin played piano and sang with a full choir. Franklin's energy and soaring **vocals** made the album a hit. *Amazing Grace* became Franklin's best-selling album!

Franklin released a popular album, *Sparkle*, in 1976. However, after that, her album sales slowed. Music was changing. A new type of music called disco was becoming popular.

ALL-STAR AUDIENCE

Several famous musicians were in the **audience** during the recording of *Amazing Grace*. Franklin's childhood influence Clara Ward was there. So was Mick Jagger, the lead singer of the Rolling Stones!

Franklin in 1976 with her oldest son, Clarence, and her youngest son, Kecalf

In 1976, Franklin and Cunningham separated. Franklin married actor Glynn Turman in 1978. During a magazine interview at the time, Franklin said that she was doing well. "Above all, I am happy," she said. But the coming years would test Franklin's happiness.

CHAPTER 7

TRAGEDY & RECOVERY

In 1979, Franklin faced a terrible tragedy. Her father was shot during a home robbery. Though he survived, he was in a **coma** until his death in 1984. Franklin had been very close to her father. Her **siblings** were not sure she could bear his death. But Franklin pushed back against their fears. She said her father had given her the strength to survive anything.

The same year her father died, Franklin divorced Turman. After her divorce and her father's death, Franklin found new meaning in her career. In 1985, she worked with popular rock and pop singers on an album called *Who's Zoomin' Who.* The album represented a new sound for Franklin. Songs such as "Freeway of Love" were fun pop hits.

Franklin's album earned her a new generation of fans. "Freeway of Love" was Franklin's biggest hit in ten years. The song also won her another Grammy. And in 1987,

Franklin became the first woman **inducted** into the Rock & Roll Hall of Fame.

Again, tragedy followed Franklin's success. Her sister Carolyn died in 1988. Her brother Cecil died a year later.

Franklin continued to record music. But it was her live performances that stood out. During every concert, Franklin reminded people why she was called the Queen of Soul.

Franklin received a Lifetime Achievement Award at the thirty-sixth Annual Grammy Awards in 1994.

CHAPTER 8

GREAT PERFORMANCES

In 1998, Franklin wowed the audience with an unexpected performance at the Grammy Awards. Opera great Luciano Pavarotti was supposed to sing. But he got sick and had to drop out at the last minute. So, Franklin agreed to sing the emotional opera song "Nessun Dorma" in his place.

Franklin had only 20 minutes to prepare. But her performance amazed listeners. Franklin moved from high to low notes with ease. Audience members shed tears as Franklin raised her arms and sang the final high note. Some call it the greatest award show performance ever.

In 2015, Franklin gave another classic performance at the Kennedy Center Honors. This annual event in Washington, DC, honors performing artists for their contributions to American **culture**. The 2015 award show honored musician Carole King, who cowrote Franklin's hit song,

I'm not going to go anywhere and just sit down and do nothing.

In 2009, Franklin sang the song "America (My Country 'Tis of Thee)" at President Barack Obama's inauguration.

"Natural Woman." Franklin performed that song during the event.

Franklin started the song playing piano. But halfway through, she walked to the front of the stage. As she sang, she pumped her arm in the air. She belted out a series of high notes. The crowd jumped to its feet. Franklin had proved that she was still a legend.

CHAPTER 9

ALL HAIL THE QUEEN

Franklin's last performance was in November 2017. The next year, Franklin's family reported that she had **cancer**. On August 16, 2018, Franklin died. She was 76 years old.

Later that month, a four-day event honored Franklin's life. It started with several public **visitation** days. Thousands of mourners came to pay their respects to Franklin. Then, there was a funeral attended by Franklin's family and friends. During the funeral, Franklin was honored by famous singers, politicians, and **civil rights activists**. The funeral was shown on TV and streamed online for the world to watch.

For 60 years, Franklin's voice awed the world. Her range and power made her stand out. But her emotion is what pulled people in. Franklin's life was

PRESIDENTIAL TRIBUTE

Former president and first lady Barack and Michelle Obama released a statement after Franklin's passing. "Every time she sang, we were all graced with a glimpse of the **divine**," they wrote. "May the Queen of Soul rest in eternal peace."

When Franklin died, fans in California left flowers and messages on her star on the Hollywood Walk of Fame.

filled with tragedies and setbacks. But she rose above them. She poured her sorrow into her music and found triumph.

TIMELINE

1942

Aretha Louise Franklin is born on March 25 in Memphis, Tennessee.

1967

Atlantic Records releases Franklin's album *I Never Loved a Man the Way I Love You*.

1985

Aretha's album, *Who's Zoomin' Who*, is released.

1961

Franklin's album *Aretha* is released.

1972

Franklin records *Amazing Grace*, a live gospel album.

1987

Franklin becomes the first woman inducted into the Rock & Roll Hall of Fame.

2009

Franklin sings at President Obama's inauguration.

2018

On August 16, Franklin dies from cancer at age 76.

1998

Franklin performs an opera song at the Grammy Awards.

2015

Franklin performs "Natural Woman" at the Kennedy Center Honors.

GLOSSARY

activist—a person who takes direct action in support of or in opposition to an issue that causes disagreement.

anthem—a song of gladness or patriotism.

audience—a group of people watching a performance.

cancer—any of a group of often deadly diseases marked by harmful changes in the normal growth of cells. Cancer can spread and destroy healthy tissues and organs.

civil rights—rights that protect people from unequal treatment or discrimination.

coma—a condition resembling deep sleep that is caused by sickness or injury.

culture—the customs, arts, and tools of a nation or a people at a certain time.

discriminatory (dihs-KRIH-muh-nuh-tor-ee)—involving unfair treatment, often based on race, religion, or gender.

divine—of, relating to, or coming directly from a god.

gospel—of or relating to religious American music containing elements of folk songs and blues.

immoral—not following certain principles of right and wrong.

induct—to admit as a member.

racism—the belief that one race is better than another.

secular—not related to religion.

segregation (seh-grih-GAY-shuhn)—the separation of an individual or a group from a larger group, especially by race.

sibling—a brother or a sister.

solo—a song or part of a song performed by a single person.

visitation—a time before a dead person is buried when people may view the body.

vocals—the parts of a song performed by the human voice.

ONLINE RESOURCES

To learn more about Aretha Franklin, please visit **abdobooklinks.com** or scan this QR code. These links are routinely monitored and updated to provide the most current information available.

INDEX